The Anglo-Saxons, Vikings and Normans

Ben Hubbard

Raintree is an imprint of Capstone Global Library Limited, a company incorporated in England and Wales having its registered office at 264 Banbury Road, Oxford, OX2 7DY – Registered company number: 6695582

www.raintree.co.uk
myorders@raintree.co.uk

Edited by Helen Cox Cannons
Designed by Cynthia Della-Rovere
Original illustrations © Capstone Global Library Limited 2018
Picture research by Tracy Cummins
Production by Kathy McColley
Originated by Capstone Global Library Limited
Printed and bound in India

ISBN 978 1 4747 5500 9 (hardback)
22 21 20 19 18
10 9 8 7 6 5 4 3 2 1

ISBN 978 1 4747 5504 7 (paperback)
23 22 21 20 19
10 9 8 7 6 5 4 3 2 1

British Library Cataloguing in Publication Data
A full catalogue record for this book is available from the British Library.

Acknowledgements
We would like to thank the following for permission to reproduce photographs: Alamy: IanDagnall Computing, 23, Ladi Kirn, 19, Roger Cracknell 01/classic, 27; Capstone: Eric Gohl, 4, 8, 15, 22; Getty Images: Bettmann, 14, CM Dixon/Print Collector, 20, Photo-12, 9, 11, Universal History Archive/UIG, 5; iStockphoto: duncan1890, 25; Shutterstock: Alexander Chaikin, 24, Andrew Roland, 26, ArtMari, Design Element, Asmus Koefoed, Design Element, chrisdorney, 28, Combatcamerauk, 10, Dave Head, 16, Good_mechanic, Design Element, 1, lovelypeace, 17, Peter Lorimer, 12, 13, 21, Pushkin, Design Element, Selenit, Cover, Skowronek, 29, StockCube, 18, VectorPot, Design Element.

We would like to thank Dr Stephen Bowman, Lecturer in History at the University of the Highlands and Islands, for his invaluable help in the preparation of this book.

Every effort has been made to contact copyright holders of material reproduced in this book. Any omissions will be rectified in subsequent printings if notice is given to the publisher.

All the internet addresses (URLs) given in this book were valid at the time of going to press. However, due to the dynamic nature of the internet, some addresses may have changed, or sites may have changed or ceased to exist since publication. While the author and publisher regret any inconvenience this may cause readers, no responsibility for any such changes can be accepted by either the author or the publisher.

CONTENTS

Some words in this book appear in bold, **like this**. You can find out what they mean by looking in the glossary.

BRITAIN AFTER THE ROMANS

In the AD 400s, Britain entered a violent and chaotic period of its history. For nearly 400 years, the country had been part of the mighty empire of Rome. The Romans had made Britain a peaceful, prosperous country and protected it against attack. But in AD 410, the Romans left Britain as their empire began to shrink and crumble. Without a central army to defend its borders, Britain was left alone and **vulnerable** to raiders and invaders.

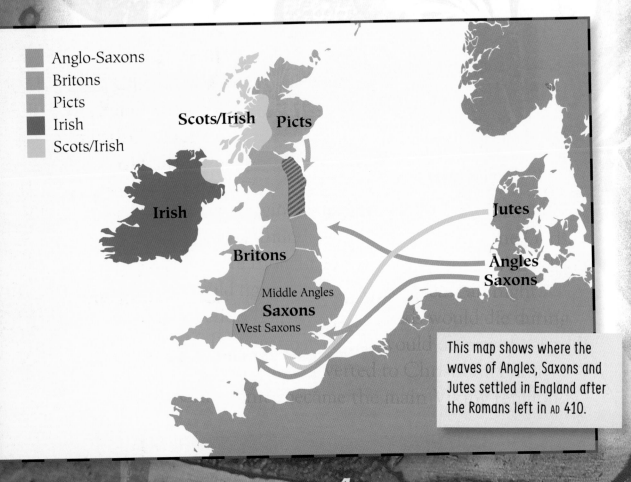

Anglo-Saxons
Britons
Picts
Irish
Scots/Irish

Scots/Irish   Picts

Irish

Britons

Middle Angles
Saxons
West Saxons

Jutes

**Angles
Saxons**

This map shows where the waves of Angles, Saxons and Jutes settled in England after the Romans left in AD 410.

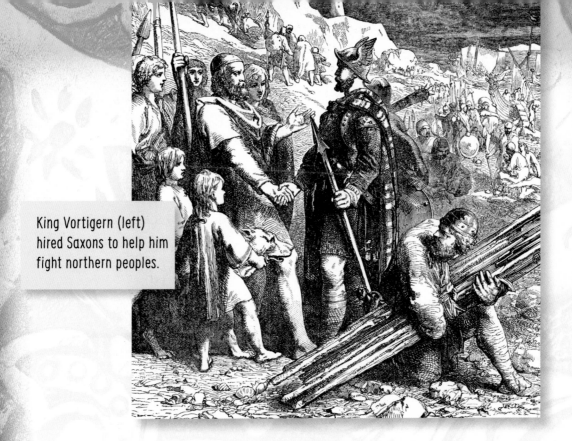

King Vortigern (left) hired Saxons to help him fight northern peoples.

Raiders and invaders

From the AD 400s, waves of Germanic warriors called Saxons, Jutes and Angles began attacking Britain. Some of the warriors simply raided British **settlements** for treasure and **loot**, while others wanted to invade the country. Some of these warriors may have already lived in Britain after serving in the Roman army. Some Saxon warriors were hired by the British leader Vortigern to protect his people and lands against attacks from the Picts and Scoti in Scotland.

How Do We Know?

After the Romans left, life in Britain became increasingly violent. There was no central government controlling the country, or written records about its history. Accounts about the Saxon **invasions**, however, were kept by monks. Bede was one of these monks. He reported that the Jutes invaded the Isle of Wight and Kent, the Angles invaded East Anglia, and the Saxons took over much of the west.

Timeline

Here is a timeline of all the events in the book. You can learn more about them as you read.

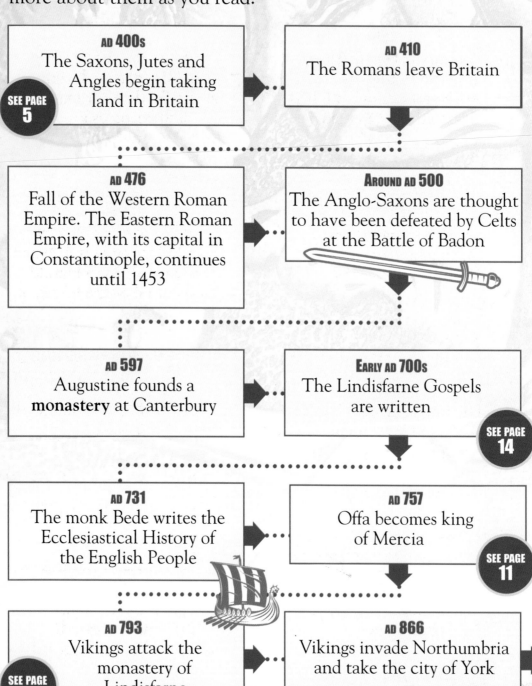

AD 400s
The Saxons, Jutes and Angles begin taking land in Britain

SEE PAGE 5

AD 410
The Romans leave Britain

AD 476
Fall of the Western Roman Empire. The Eastern Roman Empire, with its capital in Constantinople, continues until 1453

AROUND AD 500
The Anglo-Saxons are thought to have been defeated by Celts at the Battle of Badon

AD 597
Augustine founds a **monastery** at Canterbury

EARLY AD 700s
The Lindisfarne Gospels are written

SEE PAGE 14

AD 731
The monk Bede writes the Ecclesiastical History of the English People

AD 757
Offa becomes king of Mercia

SEE PAGE 11

AD 793
Vikings attack the monastery of Lindisfarne

SEE PAGE 16

AD 866
Vikings invade Northumbria and take the city of York

AD 871
Alfred the Great becomes King of Wessex

AD 878
Alfred defeats the Vikings at the Battle of Edington

SEE PAGE
18

AD 886
A **treaty** between Alfred and the Vikings awards them a part of England. It is named the Danelaw

AD 937
Athelstan defeats the British, Scots and Vikings at the Battle of Brunanburh and becomes king of England

SEE PAGE
21

1013
Swein becomes the first Viking king of England

1066
A Viking army led by Harald Hardrada is defeated by English King Harold Godwinson at the Battle of Stamford Bridge

SEE PAGE
23

1066
The English King Harold is defeated by William the **Conqueror** at the Battle of Hastings. Britain now belongs to the Normans

SEE PAGE
23

1078
The Tower of London is built

1086
The Domesday Book is completed

SEE PAGE
25

1087
William the Conqueror dies and William II becomes king of England

THE ANGLO-SAXONS

The Angles, Saxons and Jutes were invaders from what is now Germany, Holland and Denmark. Historians call these people the Anglo-Saxons. The Anglo-Saxons spoke a Germanic language and were **pagans**, which means they worshipped many gods.

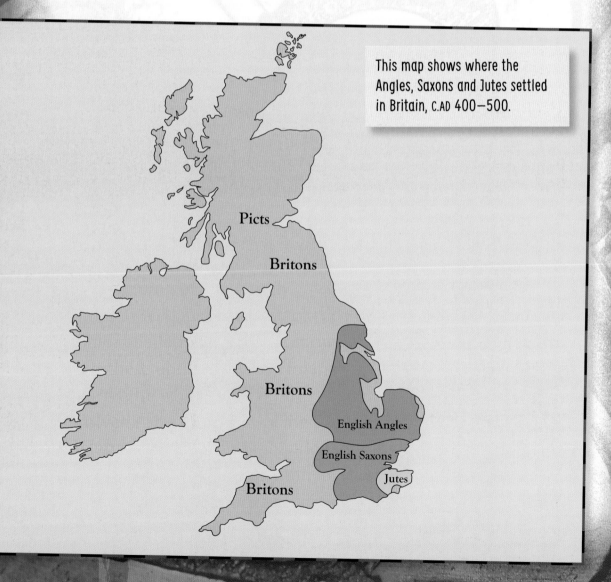

This map shows where the Angles, Saxons and Jutes settled in Britain, C.AD 400–500.

Picts

Britons

Britons

English Angles

English Saxons

Jutes

Britons

Why did they come?

The Anglo-Saxons had many reasons for coming to Britain. Some may have been driven from their homelands because of rising sea levels. Others were seeking new farmland to settle on. Some Anglo-Saxons simply found Britain an easy place to raid after the Romans left, and decided to stay permanently. It was not long before the Anglo-Saxons **conquered** the south and east of Britain. They brought with them their own beliefs, language, artwork and **culture**. Over time, they would help shape Britain into the country it is today.

After the Romans left Britain, many Celtic Britons went back to the life of their **Iron Age** ancestors. They rebuilt hill forts with stone taken from Roman towns, spoke to each other in Celtic languages instead of Latin, and revived the Celtic style of art. They used swirling Celtic circles and patterns to decorate their metalwork, and some of these goods were traded with the Anglo-Saxons. Although many Celts hated the Anglo-Saxons for taking their land, a merging of the cultures happened over time.

This gold Anglo-Saxon belt buckle was discovered in a burial ground in Sutton Hoo, Suffolk, England.

Anglo-Saxon kings and warriors

By around AD 600, the Anglo-Saxons had invaded most of today's England. They pushed any **resistance** from the Britons into Wales and Cornwall. England was then broken up into the kingdoms of Essex, Wessex, Sussex, Mercia, Northumbria, East Anglia and Kent, each with its own king. Sometimes the different Anglo-Saxon kingdoms got along, but at other times they went to war with each other. Larger kingdoms sometimes took over smaller ones.

These people taking part in a historical re-enactment give us an idea of what an Anglo-Saxon army would have looked like and the kinds of weapons they used when fighting.

Farmers and fighters

Most Anglo-Saxon men worked as farmers, but each one was required to own a spear and fight for their king at a moment's notice. An army was made up of several hundred men armed with battle-axes, spears, longbows and swords. Swords, helmets and **chain mail** armour were used by wealthy warriors. Boys were trained to fight from a young age using wooden swords.

Nobles and kings

Anglo-Saxon kings lived in large halls and lived off food collected from their villages. A king had to reward his **nobles** with feasts, weapons and jewels so they would stay loyal to him. Being a king was an unstable job and only the strongest survived for long. Offa was one of the most powerful Anglo-Saxon kings. He became King of Mercia after his cousin Aethelbald was murdered by his nobles. Offa's Dyke, a ditch between England and Wales, can still be seen today. The dyke was built as a border between Offa's kingdom and that of the Welsh.

How Do We Know?

Early Anglo-Saxons were buried with their most precious objects, which is how we know about their weapons. In Sutton Hoo in Suffolk, a burial site was discovered that contained valuable brooches, necklaces and a helmet. The grave probably belonged to King Raedwald of East Anglia.

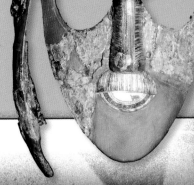

11

Anglo-Saxon life

Most Anglo-Saxons farmed a small piece of land where they grew crops, such as wheat, oats, barley and peas, and kept animals such as pigs, sheep and cows. Instead of using the Roman houses that were already there, the Anglo-Saxons made new homes with wooden frames and **thatched roofs**. They **insulated** them with mud, reeds, straw and animal dung.

This is what an Anglo-Saxon home would have looked like.

Women and girls

Life could be tough for Anglo-Saxon women and girls. Women were expected to look after the home and spend their time spinning, weaving, mending clothes, making meals and brewing drinks such as mead. Mead was an alcoholic drink made from **fermented** honey. Girls were expected to help by collecting firewood, fetching water and learning housekeeping skills. They were later expected to perform these tasks for their husbands.

The game of knucklebones was popular among Anglo-Saxon children.

Toys and games

Anglo-Saxon children played with rag dolls and wooden toys such as spinning tops, swords and ships. They also played board games and **knucklebones**. Pipes and whistles to make music have been discovered at Anglo-Saxon burial sites.

Anglo-Saxon clothes

Anglo-Saxon men and women wore long wool and linen tunics that were gathered at the waist with a belt. Men wore knee-length tunics with leggings underneath. Women's tunics went down to the ground. Cloaks fastened with large brooches were worn over people's clothes for warmth. They also wore leather shoes and gold, silver and bronze jewellery, including rings and necklaces.

Anglo-Saxon beliefs

When the Anglo-Saxons invaded Britain, they were **pagans**. They worshipped many gods, including Woden, the king of the gods, and Tiw, the god of war. In AD 597, a monk called Augustine was sent by the **Pope** in Rome to convert the Anglo-Saxons to Christianity. Over the next 100 years, Christianity became the national religion and many new churches and monasteries were built. Lindisfarne is an island in Northumberland. An illustrated manuscript of biblical gospels, or stories, was written at a **monastery** on the island.

Changing language

The Anglo-Saxon language was known as Englisc, or Old English. Many Englisc words are still in use today. Wednesday, for example, comes from 'Woden's Day', named after the Anglo-Saxon god. Tuesday is 'Tiw's Day', after Tiw, the god of war. Many Anglo-Saxon place names still exist in Britain today, too. These include Worthing in East Sussex: it was once 'Wurthingas', which means 'Wurth's people'.

This is a page from the Lindisfarne Gospels. The monks at Lindisfarne wrote it in the 8th century AD.

THE VIKINGS

The Vikings were seafaring warriors from Denmark, Norway and Sweden who began raiding the coast of Britain at the end of the AD 700s. After a period of raiding Britain, the Vikings invaded parts of the country and then settled there. Later, kings with Viking **ancestry** would fight each other for the English crown.

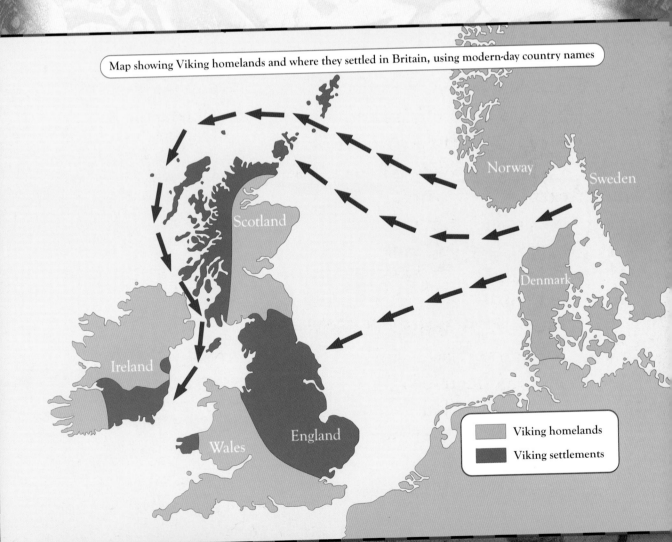

Map showing Viking homelands and where they settled in Britain, using modern-day country names

Norway

Sweden

Scotland

Denmark

Ireland

Wales

England

■ Viking homelands

■ Viking settlements

Why did the Vikings come?

One of the Vikings' first British raids was on the **monastery** at Lindisfarne in AD 793. During the raid, a **longship** full of Viking warriors **looted** the monastery's treasures and killed most of the monks living there. Viking raids on British monasteries and coastal **settlements** continued for many decades after this.

Viking warriors

The Vikings were raiding for several reasons. In Norway, there was little land to farm and men had to look for farms or ways of making a living elsewhere. Some Vikings were traders and raided when they saw a good opportunity. Most of all, Vikings believed in fighting, going on adventures and dying bravely in battle. They believed that warriors who died heroically in death would go to Valhalla, the hall of Odin, the king of their gods.

These are the remains of Lindisfarne, the first British monastery to be raided by Vikings.

The Oseberg Ship in Oslo, Norway, is one of the best **preserved** Viking longships still in existence.

Viking longships

Longships helped to make the Viking raids so successful. Longships were built with a shallow bottom that made it possible to land directly onto sandy beaches and to travel inland up rivers. By using both sails and oars, longships could travel quickly and quietly to surprise people in settlements or monasteries.

How Do We Know?

The Vikings did not have a written language, so there are no recorded details of their raiding at the time. Accounts of the Viking attacks by British monks, however, travelled all over Europe. This made many Europeans terrified of seeing the famous striped sails of a Viking longship on the horizon.

Viking battles

From the mid-AD 800s, the Vikings began attacking Britain with large armies. It was clear they wanted to invade, rather than just raid. Anglo-Saxon kings, such as Alfred of Wessex (Alfred the Great), fought the Vikings. Alfred won some victories, but in the end the Vikings forced him to sign a peace **treaty** with them. This gave the Vikings control over a large piece of England called the Danelaw.

Jorvik

One of the main towns ruled over by the Vikings was Jorvik, which is now called York. Jorvik became a busy trading town, and merchants would travel from as far away as Constantinople in Turkey to buy and sell things there. The Vikings were master craftsmen, and made many beautiful objects in their Jorvik workshops. These included ornate silver brooches, pins, rings and pendants, wooden bowls and cups, and leather boots, **scabbards** and belts.

At first the Vikings came to Britain to steal treasure and they caused destruction along the way. After a while they began to want to settle.

Viking homes

In Scandinavia, Vikings lived in longhouses, often covered with grass turf. In Britain, their houses were a mix of Viking and Anglo-Saxon styles. Jorvik houses were single-storey wooden dwellings with a **thatched roof**. The toilet was a hole in the ground outside and there was no running water. This meant the Vikings rarely washed their hands. Because of this, many Vikings in Jorvik suffered from worms in their stomach. They gave them terrible cramps and even shortened their lives.

How Do We Know?

We know about how the Vikings lived from items they left behind – including their poo! Archaeologists digging at Jorvik were excited to find **preserved** Viking poo that contained grain and hundreds of worm eggs.

In a Viking longhouse, the family usually lived in the central part. One end would house cattle and horses in the winter and the other end would be a workroom.

THE NORMANS

The Normans were originally Vikings led by a Danish chief called Rollo. In AD 912, French king Charles the Simple gave Rollo land in northern France so he would stop attacking Paris. By the 1000s, this region had become Normandy and the Vikings had become Normans. William I was Rollo's great-great-great-grandson and Duke of Normandy. In 1066, he became known as "the **Conqueror**" after he invaded England.

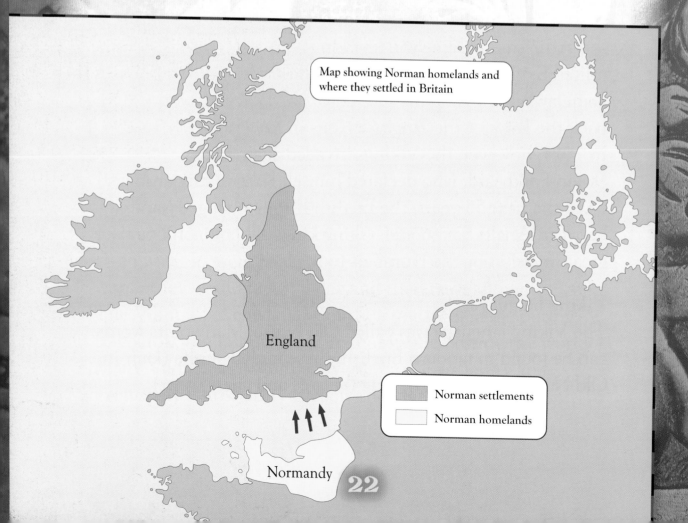

Map showing Norman homelands and where they settled in Britain

England

Normandy

Norman settlements

Norman homelands

22

1066: An important year

In 1066, there was a great struggle between three men for the crown of England. They were the Viking Harald Hardrada, William of Normandy, and King Harold Godwinson of England. All three men had Viking **ancestry**. In 1066, Harold prevented Harald's **invasion** in the north of England by defeating him at the Battle of Stamford Bridge. Around the same time, William landed his Norman army in the south. Harold marched his army all the way from Yorkshire to battle with William at Hastings in Kent. But he lost the battle and William became King of England.

This part of the Bayeux Tapestry shows Harold with the arrow in his eye.

The Tower Of London, first built by William the **Conqueror**, is a popular tourist attraction today.

ENTRY TO THE TRAITORS' GATE

Norman kings and soldiers

William crowned himself King of England on Christmas Day, 1066. He then took away the lands belonging to the Anglo-Saxons and gave them to his Norman **nobles** (known as barons). William and his barons built large castles to control their new lands and show off their power. One of the first castles to be built was the Tower of London.

The Harrying of the North

William was hated by many of the Anglo-Saxons and many people rebelled against him. However, William was quick to crush these uprisings with violence. Whenever a **rebellion** occurred he would send out his soldiers to kill all those involved. The biggest uprising came in 1069 in the north of England. Then, a combined force of English and Scottish armies attacked William. William defeated these rebels and then ordered many of the villages in the north to be destroyed.

Many villagers and their animals were slaughtered and their crops and villages burned. Widespread **famine** followed and tens of thousands of people starved to death. This was called "The Harrying of the North".

The Domesday Book

To find out what he owned in England, William sent his men around the country to take stock. They recorded who owned what and how much of everything there was, including land, homes and animals. This is how William calculated how much **tax** each person must pay him. The record was known as the Domesday Book and today it is stored in the National Archives in London.

This illustration shows monks writing the Domesday Book.

The feudal system

William used the feudal system to control England. The feudal system was how society was structured in **medieval** Britain. William was at the top of this system and below him were his barons. William's barons had to swear their loyalty to William and collect **taxes** from the local people. They also had to provide knights and men for William's army. Each baron's knights kept the peace in his lands.

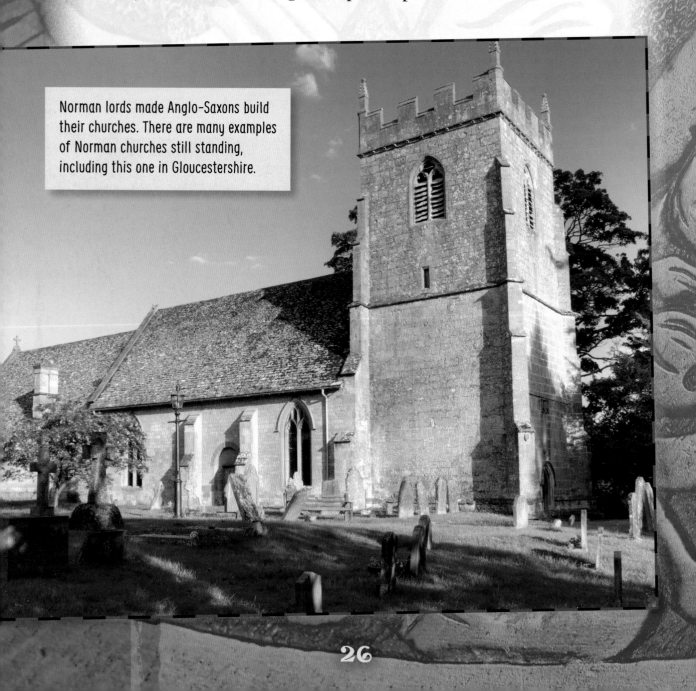

Norman lords made Anglo-Saxons build their churches. There are many examples of Norman churches still standing, including this one in Gloucestershire.

Country life

Below the knights were farmers, peasants and serfs. They had to work for the barons. Serfs were like slaves and were not paid, but instead worked for their food. Most people lived in villages on a baron's land, built near his castle. Life in a medieval village could be very hard. Peasants worked all day in the fields, even during bad weather. Sometimes a harsh winter could wipe out their crops and there was not enough to eat during the winter.

Becoming a knight

At around 7 years old, a nobleman's son could train to be a knight by becoming a page at another nobleman's house. To start with, this meant serving food at the nobleman's dinners. At the age of 12, the boy would become a squire and learn how to fight with weapons. At around 21 years old, the squire would be 'dubbed' a knight.

This man dressed up as a Norman soldier shows the "Nasal Helmet" that Normans wore. They were designed to protect the nose and face from injury.

Norman rule ends

The Norman kings were harsh and often hated by their subjects. Because they were French, however, they brought a new **culture** and trade links to Europe. This meant Britain became more connected with the rest of the world. Trade with other countries brought in goods such as wine and fine cloth that weren't easily produced in Britain. In return, Britain sent goods such as tin and wool to be sold abroad. This trade with other countries helped make Britain a wealthy nation.

The Plantagenets

The Normans did not last long as the rulers of Britain. In 1154, a new Frenchman called Henry II took the throne. Henry II belonged to a family known as the Plantagenets, who ruled England for more than 300 years. During this period, many changes took place that stopped the kings of England ruling as they pleased. Over time, governments replaced the monarchy as the leading ruling power.

Henry II was the first Plantagenet king.

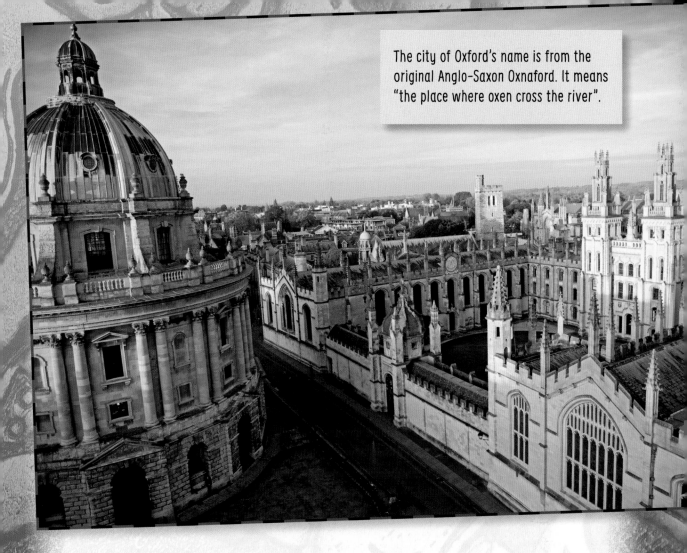

The city of Oxford's name is from the original Anglo-Saxon Oxnaford. It means "the place where oxen cross the river".

Changing language

After the Normans invaded, French became the language of the royal court, government and nobility for several centuries. This was very unfair on ordinary people, who spoke English. Over time, however, many French words found their way into the language. These included fashion (*facon* in French), beef (*beouf*) and cauldron (*chaudron*). These French words joined the Anglo-Saxon and Old Norse words, which became part of today's English. Modern English is a mixture of languages brought by the settlers and invaders of Britain over history.

Glossary

ancestry person's family or people from the past

bard storyteller and singer who told stories about history and mythology

chainmail armour made of lots of metal rings joined together

conquer take control of an area or country by force

culture customs and beliefs of a group of people

famine extreme shortage of food

ferment process that turns some sugars and fruits into alcohol

insulate pad walls with materials to keep heat in a home

invasion taking over a place or country by force

Iron Age period in history that lasted between around 800 BC and AD 43

knucklebones game played by throwing and catching knucklebones

longship long, narrow warship used by the Vikings

loot steal goods or valuable items from a person or place

medieval relating to the Middle Ages, from about 1000 to 1453

monastery place where monks live

nobles people at the top of society

pagan person believing in many gods and goddesses, instead of only one god

Pope leader of the Roman Catholic Church

preserved kept whole, safe or in existence

rebellion fight against a ruler or ruling group

resistance people who try to stop something or someone using force

scabbard cover for a sword

settlement place where people make their homes

tapestry piece of embroidered fabric with patterns or pictures

tax money or goods paid by people to a king or government

thatched roof roof made of straw and reeds

treaty written agreement

vulnerable left open to the possibility of being harmed or attacked

FIND OUT MORE

Books

Anglo-Saxon Sites (Historic Places of the United Kingdom), Nancy Dickmann (Raintree, 2018)

The Viking and Anglo-Saxon Struggle for England (Early British History), Claire Throp (Raintree, 2016)

Viking Sites (Historic Places of the United Kingdom), Nancy Dickmann (Raintree, 2018)

Websites

www.bbc.co.uk/guides/z3s9j6f
Everything you could want to know about the Normans is on this BBC site, with helpful video clips included.

www.bbc.co.uk/schools/primaryhistory/anglo_saxons
Learn more about the Anglo-Saxons on this BBC website.

www.bbc.co.uk/schools/primaryhistory/vikings
Learn more about the Vikings on this BBC website.

www.show.me.uk/topicpage/Anglo-Saxons.html
This website has information and activities on the Anglo-Saxons from museums around the country.

Places to visit

If you want to visit some of the places in this book, find out more by looking up the following websites:

The Jorvik Viking Centre in York
www.jorvikvikingcentre.co.uk

The National Trust
www.nationaltrust.org.uk

The National Trust for Scotland
www.nts.org.uk

English Heritage
www.english-heritage.org.uk

INDEX